'M' IS FOR MIRROR

FIND THE HIDDEN PICTURES

Duncan Birmingham

A is for Astronomer, who studies the moon

B is for Balloon, drifting high in the sky

C is for Clown, who is happy today

D is for Drummer, who drums out the beat

E is for Everest, a mountain of men

F is for Face, mysterious and pale

G is for Gift, some flowers for the lady

H is for Handshake, they decide to make friends

I is for Insect, with delicate wings

J is for Jaws, which swallow the trainer

K is for Keeper, with tightly shut box

L is for Lamp, it lights a small room

M is for Mirror, he admires his fine clothes

N is for Neptune, the King of the sea

O is for Ostrich, which looks straight ahead

P is for Pyramids, the explorer is seeking

Q is for Questions, how old is each child?

R is for Robot, now ready to walk

S is for Sisters, who dance round the bull

T is for Teddy, alone in the sand

U is for Umbrella, which is shady and cool

V is for Valley, no houses in sight

W is for Whistle, he's piping a tune

X^y is for Xylophone, played with great glee

Z is for Zoom, away to the stars

MIRROR ANSWERS

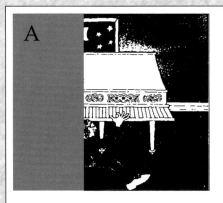

A

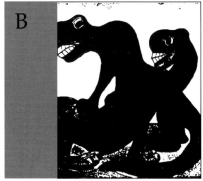

B

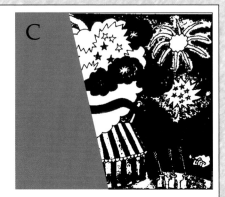

C

D

E

F

G

H

I

These diagrams show where the mirror has to be placed and which side to look from.
The area marked in purple reveals the hidden picture!

These diagrams show where the mirror has to be placed and which side to look from.
The area marked in purple reveals the hidden picture!

S

T

U

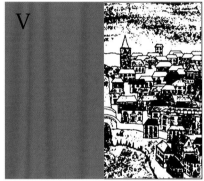

V

W

Xy

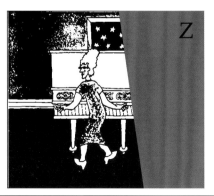

Z

MIRROR
ANSWERS

A

GLUE THE BACK OF THE MIRROR HERE

B

THE MIRROR STAND

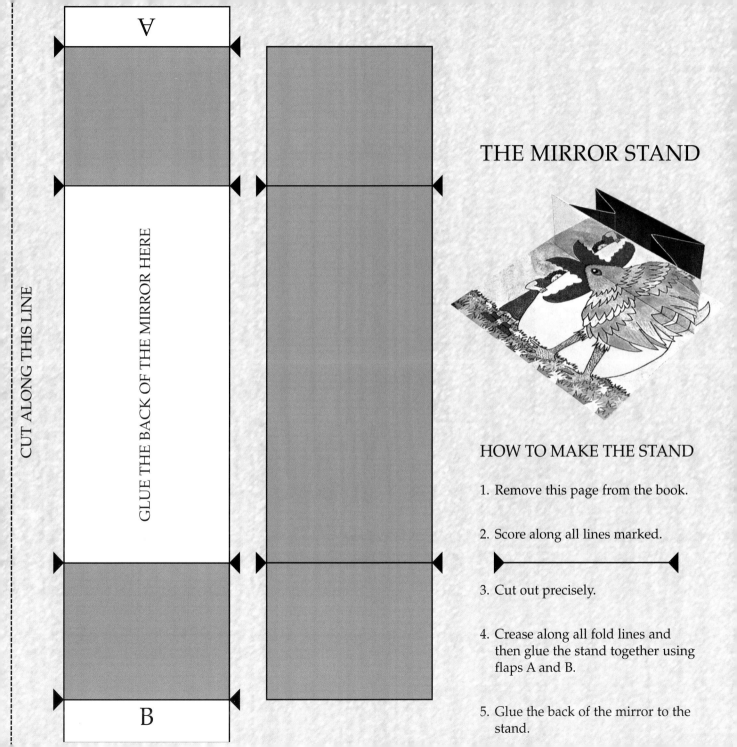

HOW TO MAKE THE STAND

1. Remove this page from the book.

2. Score along all lines marked.

3. Cut out precisely.

4. Crease along all fold lines and then glue the stand together using flaps A and B.

5. Glue the back of the mirror to the stand.

A

B